From Barry

by

Chris Robillard

First Edition.

[signature]

7th December 2016

Devon Matters Publishing

First Published in 2015 by

Devon Matters Publishing
8 St Pauls Close
Bovey Tracey
TQ13 9JD

Paperback ISBN 978-0-9934451-0-1

Designed by Antony Evans Look3dstudio

Printed and bound in the UK by
Short Run Press

This book is dedicated to the Italian people who showed great courage, humanity and bravery in assisting allied prisoners' of war.

Love and thanks to
Barbara, Lisa, Lucy, Kate and Wendy
our Italian friends
Stella, Mariella and Flavia

David's Story

CHAPTER 1

THE EARLY YEARS

My mother, Blanche, left school at the age of 12 - as did most of my family. After working at Torbay Hospital at the outbreak of the war, she met my Canadian father at Torbay Hospital. He had been wounded in France and had come to Devon for medical treatment. They married in 1916.

My father was a French Canadian lumberjack from Quebec Province.

He was called up at 17 and joined the Canadian Forestry Regiment and was injured near the Somme in France. His regiment were based at Stover near Newton Abbot and he met my mother while recovering from his injuries.

In 1917 my brother Bill was born and 13 months later I arrived. We lived in a downstairs room in St. James' Road - talk about overcrowding! It was a terrible situation. Nevertheless we stayed there until my Aunt Emily died when I was 2. Once old granny died a year later we were allowed a bedroom to live in - my mother, father and us two children. My sister was born 4 years later. I was about 5 years old when we attained a council house in Hele with facilities (bathroom and toilet etc) and we went to live there.

I'd started school at 3 years old and my brother was 4. We went to St. James' School – even after we moved to Hele. It was a long way away but we had to make the march every morning to school.

During that period of the war my grandmother had been working in a laundry at the back of Parkfield Road where she fell and broke her hip. As medical attention was not available then, the hip re-joined itself but left her disabled for the rest of her life. Therefore my mother used to go down and look after her. We had to do a 3 mile trip to take the washing to my mother and then of course we had to bring it back the same way. The roads were not tarmacked in those days and the amount of traffic was very sparse. It was mainly horse & trap traffic. There were few buses around until the 1930's and then we were able to take the old steam bus up and down the Teignmouth Road.

I remember walking to school, having lunch at my grandmother's and then walking back to Hele at half past 4. In summer it was not too bad, but in the winter it was quite a long trek for little legs. However, we survived it.

My sister went to school at Westhill which opened in 1926. It was quite a distance but nonetheless was

The Strand Torquay 1919

closer than St. James's. As we progressed in school it became clear to me that I was about a year ahead of my class. The school wanted me to take the grammar school examinations but I knew full well my parents didn't have the money to send me there. I knew it was 6 guineas a term, if you passed the necessary examination. I passed the examination but having no facilities to go, I went to Upton School. This was following the family tradition with Bill (my brother), Arthur (my uncle) and Charlie also going there.

Our father, being a 'foreigner', found it difficult to attain work. Therefore he had to get work wherever he possibly could. It wasn't until the 1930's that he got on his feet and took up the job that he most wanted which was landscape gardening, horticulture and tree surgery. He started this in about 1935 / 1936 which was hard work for him but nevertheless he succeeded in it.

Bill left school at 14 and went to work in a bakery. After 12 months he took a 4 year bakery apprenticeship. I left school at 14 and my first job was 5 shillings a week peeling potatoes in a potato peeling factory. I lasted about a fortnight. I moved on to a temporary position in the Co-op which after 2 months turned into a permanent position. I remained in the Co-op employment for the next 50 years.

When we were youngsters, being poor was something we had to get used to, we used to have to find ways of getting spending money. One way of doing it was to get bedsteads. We would take the bars off and take them up to the concrete works for a penny or tuppence for each bedstead or iron. We got quite a bit of money so we were able to buy the odd fish & chips or bit of fruit.

At 8 years old I was given a pass to the recreation ground to watch rugby. I fell in love with rugby and as a youngster I used to go down there every Saturday. I got invited to take the board around with the program numbers on etc. Eventually I was given a job selling programmes which I remained in until I left school at 14. At the county matches we were able to make quite a bit of money.

Saturdays used to be a day of chores (especially the mornings). We used to get the groceries for my grandmother from the shops and get all she wanted from the town. We would also collect papers for my uncle who had a paper round on Sunday. You got a penny for each paper and comic. The delivery used to complement my uncles' wages. I assisted with this until I was 17 because I wanted to learn how to drive a car. I drove my grandmother's car on the delivery - delivering papers and learning to drive at the same time.

My grandmother always owned a car ever since I was about 3 years old and right up until her death. So she was never really poor. The family lived-in for a very low rent. The income came from the men (Arthur & Walter) who both worked in the brickworks. Bill worked for Webbers instead. First of all he worked at Davies the construction workers. He was always dealing with motorists so naturally he ended up owning a car and motorbikes. There were always motorbikes around there.

As far as I'm concerned, my mother was poor. You knew they were struggling. They were not poor enough to need soup from the soup kitchens unlike some of the others.

When I first worked down at the Co-op, I started with the usual as a butcher boy. We were invited to go to college to do necessary training for our job. I took up the opportunity and went to South Devon College which had just been built. I did the hygiene training for my job. I also learnt about slaughtering. My half days used to be spent down on the farm with the animals, purely voluntarily, taking the sheep dogs out and rounding sheep up. I enjoyed being there. However this was training for my future ahead, it was a job I liked doing and I got a great satisfaction from it.

Later in my teens, I joined a youth group in St. Marychurch (League of Youth) and I started and chaired a youth group with the Co-op. I was there until the beginning of the war. They were a very successful group and we travelled around several towns in South Devon with different Co-operative groups with dancing and different subjects. And then, of course, came the war effort.

CHAPTER 2

JOINING UP

When I was 20 I had to join up. So I decided to stay with some friends in London and that's when I met Pat (my future wife) in 1938, it was a couple of days before her birthday. So it's 60 years ago that we met. We had a few evenings out together. The following Christmas she came down to Torquay and spent the week in Torquay with me. The next time I saw her was in May 1939, from then I didn't see her again until June 1945. The main reason being was that all leave and holidays were stopped in Torquay (you couldn't travel because of the war).

I waited until July to be called up but it was subsequently cancelled within 24 hours. I was called up too late. I was called up again in September but it was put back for a month. Eventually in October, I was in the Army and began my training. It would have been impossible to get away for a holiday after that.

Pat was working in London for the government and they moved their offices to Blackpool. In no time at all, she was far away in Blackpool and I was still in Exeter training. In 1940, I passed out from the training centre and most of the men were moved to the Royal West Kent's regiment (The King's Own) and moved to France. However I was accepted and sent with a convoy to Norway. We were on the boat ready to set sail from

Portsmouth and the word came through that Norway had been invaded by the Germans. Therefore I never made it to Norway.

I came back to Salisbury Plain for about a month and was then moved to Plymouth where there was the potential of promotion. I took up the rear guard of Plymouth in about June when Dunkirk had already happened. The trials of invasion were going on by the Germans and we were there to protect Plymouth. No leave was available and you couldn't go anywhere - it was a case of 'do as you were told'!

I joined the Passive Air Defence Corps which was looking after victims (first aid etc.) when it was necessary. I drove an ambulance in the air raids when the rest of the ambulances were completely exhausted. We used our own ambulance as reserve.

At the end of 1940, I had been working on the petrol side of the engineering side of the army. I was put on draught to be sent abroad. Our O.C at the time, asked if I wanted to defer it as he could arrange it. But I said no, I would take my fate as it came. So in 1940 I was sent to Barry. Just after Christmas in 1940, I took the train to Liverpool and sailed out – our destination unknown. It turned out to be the Middle East.

This is one of the best kept secrets of the Army. They didn't tell us where we were going but they fitted us out with pith helmets, shorts and khaki shirts and stockings to parade in. Nobody knew where we were going but with all of this equipment it was pretty obvious we were going to a hot country.

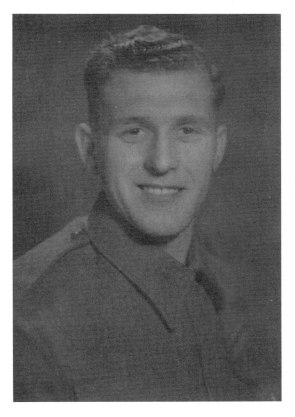

David joining up

CHAPTER 3

JOURNEY TO EGYPT

We sailed as soon as we arrived in Liverpool. Our ship
HMS Sameria (Troop ship) had to be thoroughly
checked for incendiary bombs as we had been bombed
that evening. The following day we sailed to Belfast and
then onto Glasgow. From there we went out into the
Atlantic. Our first port of call was Freetown, in Sierra
Leone where it was very hot. We stayed there for
about 4 days and then we sailed again out to the
Atlantic and down to Capetown. We spent a couple of
days there, then on to Durban for a week where we
replenished and refuelled.

HMS Ramillies

The convoy was 40 strong. **HMS Ramillies** (Battleship Class) was our escort ship. We sailed for Egypt through the Indian Ocean where the Ramillies left us. We sailed the rest of it practically on our own until we reached Suez. At Suez, we disembarked and were put into a camp called Genifa (Jifjafah) up on the Suez Canal. We stayed there for about 2 or 3 days and went through several tests to find out if we had the necessary qualifications. I was posted to a petrol depot in El Qirsch on the Suez Canal about 5 miles from **Izbali**.

The first thing that happened was that I was stripped of my Corporal stripes but that's what you expect when you join a new company. I was given the job of looking after the ledgers of stocks for petrol, oil and lubricants. This was quite exciting really to start with, but as the summer wore on it became very difficult because men were falling like flies from malaria. Our unit was depleted by 50% and therefore we were doing jobs that really we weren't trained to do. I was doing the sergeant's and corporal's jobs as I was the only one left out of an office of 5 due to malaria. **Chris Melville** (a sergeant in the administration block) and I were the only two who had come through the disease without being hospitalised and therefore remained on the unit. Everyone else had to join other units as the malaria had kept them away from our unit for more than a few months.

At the end of 1941, I was called up to be moved to Tobruk to take over the petrol depot there. My officer, **Major Guildford** opposed it, saying that it wasn't right to be singularly moved to another unit in a war zone without further training (as did many). However, I said no and agreed to take the job with the 115 company in Tobruk where I took over the stocks, ledgers and all the buying for the oils and petrols.

CHAPTER 4

TOBRUK

During the month of June a letter was received from the Commander of 10th Corp saying that it was necessary to withdraw the eighth army for regrouping. Only key personnel would remain in Tobruk, the rest would be evacuated. Ninety days were mentioned before we would be relieved. The following day over one hundred of our unit were evacuated from base leaving us with just twenty five men. This depleted our company from 102 down to a skeleton crew of 25 men. 25 of us were doing the jobs of over 100 men. It was obvious to me, having control of all the stock books in the Petrol Depot that we only had sufficient supplies for about thirty days, so, of course, seeds of doubt were planted immediately. A type of rationing was imposed, units were issued two thirds of their quota.

Another coded message was received that ten of us (my name included) were – if Tobruk fell – to make for a point five miles up the coast to a rendezvous with map reference and we would be picked up by M T B from the Navy. Everything pointed to the fact that we were going to be over-run.

Now cut off, we were left under these circumstances for about a month.   The week before Tobruk fell on 21st June, the bombing and shelling from the Germans became more intense; they did as they wished. We had no position to hold off their strikes of dive–bombing and low level machine gunning.

Our petrol depot was situated in a wadi quite near to the perimeter and most of the shelling went over our heads. We had two tents as offices, but by this time we had to move into the caves and the men into rat holes for sleep.

The attacks were now more frequent and intense. On Saturday morning, June 22, the tanks had broken through and entered the town. We saw the heavy artillery retreat and the A.A guns. Later in the afternoon we saw the Germans capture the field artillery HQ and the R.A.O.C. Our cookhouse received a direct hit and the office underground received a hit. Two of us were in there and it took four hours to dig us out. Nevertheless no one was injured. We had kept in touch with GHQ until 2 o'clock and then the phone went dead.

By six o'clock there were fires blazing all around and we decided to try and break out. Two of our trucks went out at different times and both returned after being machine gunned. We were being shelled as well – we thought by our own troops across the hill. Our offices (tents) were destroyed and a couple of petrol depots caught on fire. Action was taken to destroy as much of the supplies as possible and put the vehicles and M/guns out of action.

At night I took 10 of our company to make for a point in Tobruk called the Cherry Tree, where we'd be picked up by the E-Boat (or Torpedo Boat) and taken back to base to continue our work. At 8 o'clock at night we tried to make a push through the back roads to get to this point. But it was impossible as we came under heavy fire from the Germans.

By then it was dark so we went into the officers' cave. The amount of drink the officers had amazed me - whisky, brandy, sherry and port. But the men couldn't muster a cup of water. The officers shared the drink with the men. Our first thought was to get drunk and forget our situation by drowning our sorrows. Not so. I drank a bottle of brandy (having never tasted it before) and a ½ bottle of whisky. But I was still sober and as frightened as hell.

At two o'clock in the morning I approached the 2nd in command for the order "Every man for himself". He refused. Two of us had a plan to escape. He finally gave the order at 4.30am when it was light.   All the weapons had to be destroyed. We were doing this when the Germans came up to take us. As we were on the perimeter of Tobruk, it had taken until the Sunday morning, 22 June, for us to be captured. To say that our capture was very traumatic is putting it very mildly, it was more than that.

When the German patrol came, our captain, Captain Watts, gave me the keys to the safe instructing me to destroy all the personnel documents and money (£30,000). I slipped by the Germans and put the files into an old oil drum and set it on fire. They say money burns – this certainly did. A German officer came running and pointing his revolver at me telling me to get out of the way – he flicked open a can thinking it was water and poured it over the flames. It happened to be paraffin, for a moment the flames went down then with an explosion burst into flames again – burning all our records.

All the monthly records had been with us and they'd all been destroyed in that fire. It meant that there were no known records of us for 6 months. After the war, the Army told me they still had my all records - which of course, I knew full well they didn't. (We weren't paid for those 6 months and money had been taken from my pay – something I now choose to forget).

We were rounded up and marched seven miles to the airport which they used as a P.O.W enclosure. We had no water, food, clothing or anything. At 2pm that day the last of the defending groups marched in. The 4th Indian Division with 2 Scottish regiments held out until midday then with bagpipes playing they marched into the compound. It was very inspiring at the time, but very soon the wind would be taken out of their bagpipes.

We were there for three days with no food or water in the tremendous heat. There was no cover whatsoever, most of us were accustomed to the searing heat, but a few hadn't been in the Middle East for more than 2 months and they just couldn't stand up to it. You couldn't speak or anything.

As far as we were concerned the British Army had told us that no aircraft was able to land at Tobruk airport and the British air force didn't use it at all. However the Germans landed on the second day with planes carrying supplies of troops and food etc.

On the fourth day lorries came to move us out in convoys of six. We first of all went to Deriva and then on to a place called Sinai Flats, Timini for 3 or 4 days. It was the salt flats, if you dug down you could get good water, but it was mainly salt water. All kinds of gimmicks we used to get the salt out of the water but to no avail.

We were then transported to **Benghazi,** a more up-to-date prison compound with barbed wire around it. At last we had an issue of water ½ mug per person per day. This was for drinking, washing, shaving and everything else, hence my thoughts on water. I saw one of the water tanks, outside the barbed wire leaking just a drop every 2 seconds or so. That night I crawled through the wire and held a mess tin under the drip for about three hours, I can tell you it was worth it. There was a lot of thieving going on inside the compound, you had to carry everything. Punishment by the Germans was severe. They tied a man to a telegraph post for 24 hours, he would be only wearing shorts and as the sun went around him he would get burned. I saw several men punished this way and had mixed feelings about it.

Tobruk under attack

CHAPTER 5

JOURNEY TO NAPOLI

About a fortnight later we were taken to the docks and put aboard ships to Tripoli. Straight down into the hold where you had to stand, no room to sit. We were put in like sardines and you just couldn't move. Three days on there, they allowed ten men at a time to go to the toilets, so some on board would never make it. I tell you, the conditions were terrible. When I went up I spoke to the man counting, in an effort to confuse him and succeeded. 12 of us got up and ten were counted, so it meant hiding on deck for 2 nights and 2 days. We succeeded because the crew were Italian merchant seamen and they really didn't bother much. They also gave us a bit of food when the Germans weren't around. I hid in a coil of rope at night using it as shelter from the cold. By the time we reached Naples, about 12 men had not survived the trip.

Naples came as a relief after 3 days in the 'Rosa Pena'. We arrived to the sight of the volcano Mount Vesuvius erupting. We filed through the fort and were given a small loaf of bread which we found out later had to last for 3 days. We were able to fill our water bottles which was important. We were then put onto a railway cattle truck with 50 others with a grid window on each side.

We were about a day and a half travelling to our final destination Camp No. 64 in Lucca, Tuscany. When we arrived there were rainstorms…….rain rain rain, it was terrible. We later discovered that Tuscany and especially Lucca were known for their rainfall. We marched from the station to the camp and were immediately split into platoons of 30 men with an NCO in charge.

Our conditions were the worst possible and for about 3 or 4 months we endured horrible times. We were slimmed down, weak and fatigued. Our rations were 100g of bread a day and that was the lot, bit of soup perhaps.

The tents had a back and a top with the front open. Twigs and branches of trees were spread out on the floor with your sleeping arrangements, we were four between each hole 2 yards apart. It's practically impossible to describe the conditions. There was mud throughout the camp and water running through the tents; it meant you were wet-through day and night.

It was here that I met an old Coop work colleague of mine, Bill Locke. He recognised me and naturally spoke with his broad Devonshire accent - that was proof enough of his identity.

Dysentery was rife. The toilet was a simple hole over an open pit and with the strength of many men diminishing; the fear of falling in was prominent. There was an average of six deaths a day. The Italians had a cart with two coffins on the back drawn by a horse. The bodies were put in the coffins – taken to a mass grave, the floor of the coffins was opened, the bodies dropped out, and then they returned to the camp for more – the same coffins all the time. Several protests were made about the conditions generally, but at this particular time of the war we were in no position to protest - what with the allies at El Alamein and the bombing of the UK, you can just imagine how the morale of the inmates was. The Italian authority sensed this and behaved in such a manner as if we counted for nothing.

Escape was in the minds of most, but we just did not have the strength to do anything. We were told that Red Cross parcels would arrive. We were there four months and I can remember two issues of parcels – not one each as intended but one to be shared amongst 4 men.

Men were trying to eat grass, roots and twigs – anything but it only added to the dysentery. Several men were shot and killed trying to escape; actually it was more like committing suicide. An escape committee was formed to try to dissuade some of the silly acts which could only end in death. Everything was tried to try to raise morale in the camp but hunger was at the foremost. One day an issue of carrots was made, all one could hear was the crunch of carrots followed two hours later by stomach ache. Almost a week later a batch of onions came in – one onion each – the effects weren't as bad as the carrots but made the toilets smell a lot worse!

News of the progress of the war was very hard to come by. One could notice the different attitudes of the Italians towards us relating to the war situation. After September when the big push was made from El Alamein through the desert, the Italians treated us a little better and one could sense the Allies success. I was trying to learn Italian and on speaking to one of the guards he was able to tell me a little news. Many men in the camp were doing the same, so we decided we would pool our information and try and put out a bulletin on it so as to pass it on. At least it gave us a little bit of hope to know our troops were advancing again.

CHAPTER 6

MOVING TO MACERATA

In November we were told we were moving to a more permanent camp. The walk to the station was about 2 miles – the majority of us were just too weak to make it. I struggled along helping one of the unfortunate compatriots as were many others. We reached the station and there were piles of collapsed bodies.

Back in the cattle trucks and on to **Macerata (Camp 152)** near the East Coast close to Ancona which is a port on the coast. We were strip searched before we went into the camp. Several men in my platoon of 30 had knives etc. which would be confiscated. However I decided to bluff my way through. I put all the knives, tools, etc. into my bag. I told my men to follow my orders to the letter. When it came to us, I saluted the NCO who called out the men for a quick inspection. I saluted the officers, thanked them and walked through without being searched. It worked and all the men were relieved to have their possessions intact. I wouldn't like to say how fast my heart was beating! The punishment would have been very severe if I was caught.

The conditions at **Macerata** were better. We were put in a big building but still the food was scarce. It needs a lot to explain the endurance of it but nonetheless, we survived.

The camp in Macerata was divided into 3 parts, No 1 had 4,000 inmates, No 2, where I was, had 2,500 and no 3 had 2,000. There were 180 men in each section. I was the corporal in charge of one section. Our part of the camp was in the middle. The exercise field covered the 3 compounds so we could meet in the field. At night, everyone was confined to their own compound and search lights and machine guns were trained on the road throughout the night.

Bill Locke was actually in my platoon and was on the bunk behind me. We did meet several people from South Devon and spent hours chatting, really about nothing. On Christmas Eve – Bill was taken into the camp hospital and he was very ill. I was able to visit him, but he was so weak with a poisoned leg. He looked a wreck but he did survive. He remained there for about 2 weeks before returning to the camp. We remained in contact until the late 1990s.

It was a question of survival of the fittest in the prison camp. I did a fatigue job in the camp with 12 men. We went in on fatigues every day, purely and simply to try and get any kind of food we could use; for example, small apples from the trees or potatoes that weren't quite ready or cabbage leaves ……..anything, anything to eat in order to survive.

Rumours were passed around every day and although one would like to believe them they all ended up as wishful thinking. It was on this camp that we met a PO from the Navy called Bert Flagg who incidentally was a relation of Len Pollard from Torquay. He told us he had a list of names which he had to evacuate from Tobruk, my name was among them. He told us he just took some men on board and got shot at by a German U Boat. There were several casualties, so perhaps I was lucky.

A British Officer in another part of the camp had said he would grow a beard and only shave it off when the Germans were ousted from North Africa. You can imagine the cheers when he walked by, about 100 yards away under escort clean shaven.

Activities in the prison camp go on day and night, tin bashing it was called. Some inmates were able to put their skills into turning empty tins into many things – such as fires with a fan. Some examples are displayed in the war museums in London. Brewing tea was a great occupation. The difficulty was getting fuel with which to boil the water. Some used the struts from their beds – old socks – anything that we could burn. One day the Italians brought in a wooden ladder and went up on the roof. Whilst up there, the ladder was taken and demolished in no time. Then a cart pulled by a donkey was in the camp. The cart was made of metal but one of the inmates saw the spokes were made of wood. At lunch time, the Italians went out leaving the cart and, hey presto, the spokes disappeared. If they had left the donkey I expect it would have gone the same way. It did create a laugh at the time but of course it meant more roll calls and searches to try and find the culprits.

It was during January, 1943 that all the naval personnel were being repatriated back to England after a deal had been made with the Germans – why? I don't know. But Jack Stembridge of Barton Hill Road, Torquay was one of them and he was able to tell me later they were taken by Italian ship to Turkey and there transferred on to English ships whilst the German sailors left the British ship and entered the Italian ships.

Every time a new intake arrived they were quizzed for information – usually they had been transferred from another camp and had no other information than we had. However, I did start learning Italian and tried to communicate with the Italian guards. I asked them how the war was progressing and they said the Allies were making slow progress in Italy. This was news – we never knew anything of the landing. After this I spoke to them quite often. A bulletin was arranged between the three compounds and one section was well ahead with the news, they had built a wireless set and got information from that.

The only thing I bartered myself, was for a book. Many inmates had books and naturally would only charge for a book they hadn't read. I made an exchange for the book "Strawberry Roan" it wasn't very popular but it was reading matter – from then on I was able to improve the standard of books.

Red Cross parcels were a very sore point. The issue was to be one per person per week. We were fortunate to get one a month divided between two persons. The welcome sight of tea and milk at least. If you can make a brew the hunger pains are subdued for a while. The rations were as follows that is from the Italians – 8am 1 mug of black substance which they called coffee – 12 mid-day loaf the size of a bun weighing 150 grams and an issue of cheese – hardly believable the amount was actually half the size of a sugar cube. What we did was for each platoon to have the ration for 4 sections a day therefore each man had a reasonable amount every 4 days. At 5 o'clock a stew which was mostly vegetables – cabbage leaves, carrots and onions – one mug full per man – mostly water. Some of the inmates got double or treble rations for helping the Italians with the administration of the camp such as cookhouse fatigues. I was totally against it. However I saw some of these men become potbellied through the extra stew they consumed whilst I kept my "slim-like" figure.

It is very difficult to retain a self discipline when you are actually starving, but the majority of the men kept very close to the rules "Don't help the enemy"! One day the Italians came in for 50 men to help on the docks – no one went from our section – I can't speak for the others. There was only one water tap running in the section and the queue was constant night and day drawing water. There were showers there, in six months I can only remember being able to use them once – then the water was cold and only a dribble. Having watched some of the prisoner of war films on television I began to wonder if they are true or not. 'Tenko' was the only series close to the conditions we lived in.

Swiss officials of the Red Cross arrived in April and relayed terms of the Geneva Convention on Prisoners of War. They weren't very helpful to us but insisted we had to do agricultural work. The officials listed many other jobs which in turn we rejected as they were considered helpful to the enemy.

Macerata

CHAPTER 7

MOVE TO ZEVIO

Things began to move and many men were sent to different camps – my turn came in May 1943. All the men with the surname initial P and R were called out from our section – the next day transported to a camp called Zevio 48K about 30 miles from Verona.

To many men it was a hardship because they had their respective pals or friends and were forced apart. To the average person it may not mean a lot but when your resistance is low – the body weak – it meant a lot to them. For my part it was not so hard – I had preferred to go solo. My friend at Camp 153 was called Harry Pomfret – a married man with two daughters from Lancashire. I had helped him over many a hurdle and he was sorry to see me go.

We were moved as a working party of 147 for agricultural work. It was the only work we were allowed to do. Any other work you could refuse (not that we were offered anything else). It was purely agricultural work down on a farm.

At the time we were put into a building which was absolutely flea ridden – not very pleasant; although we found out we wouldn't be in there very long.

144 of us formed 12 platoons of 12 men (one WCO and eleven others). plus one man to oversee the camp, one man to clean the camp and one man to do the administration. There were 148 in the camp – one leader and three to cover any sickness. Twelve of us had to go out every day to work. I was in charge of no.1 squad and we worked at a farm.

We arose at 5 o'clock and dispatched to our place of work down at the farm at 6 o'clock in the morning. As it was a five mile walk, we'd get there about 7 to 7.30am. Starting work at 8am with an hour's lunch at midday, we then started work again from 1pm. At 6pm we would march the 5 miles back to camp to that delightful watery stew and then do your washing before going to bed.

This routine happened seven days a week with no extra rations. More significantly, they made sure the men weren't together. The fields were about a mile long but the 12 men were interspersed with 12 women - one in between each of us so we couldn't talk to each other. But the women were very good and sometimes used to give us nubs of bread and little bits of cheese which we accepted with great gratitude. They didn't have much themselves but we managed to keep going. We got quite a relationship with them and there are several things that happened at camp (which aren't worth mentioning here).

We found all kinds of ways to increase our supply of food – the pigs' potatoes were one source, small new potatoes we would dig out from under the plants – beans, peas, herbs, corn on the cob at its youngest stages. It was at this farm we were able to weigh ourselves and it was a bit of a shock to me as I weighed just 8 stone 4 pounds – when captured, I had scaled 14 and a half stone.

The main work was a back-breaking job of hoeing the maize and root crops. As we were separated as a female between each male, the girls worked fast and so that we could keep up with them they did most of our work as well.

Every week the barriers were lifted in the rice field and the water let out so that we could go in and weed the rice – a very sticky job. It's surprising the amount of fish left stranded amongst the rice, the women collected these as tomorrow's dinner. Our feet felt like slimy sponges!

My knowledge of Italian improved and I was able to have a conversation with the Italians. Speaking to the land owner one day, I was surprised to hear that we were forced onto him as labour and he had to pay the Italian Government the same wage for each prisoner as he would have to pay civilian workers. Believe me, we weren't worth it! I do think this is where my feelings towards the Italians changed. He was paying all this money for us, and we had been doing everything we could to sabotage his farm.

We'd arrive back at camp and cook our tea or dinner. We would light a fire and cook over it. We never had corned beef but a kind of meat loaf that came in the Red Cross parcels. Red Cross parcels were very welcome.

CHAPTER 8

ITALIANS WITHDRAW FROM THE WAR

It was towards the end of July that the first news about Badoglio came through to us. Rumours were that he was going to negotiate terms with the Allies. We had a meeting and decided we must act before the Germans, knowing full well that we would be transported to Germany if anything like that happened. The Camp Commandant was approached and arranged a meeting with the 123 NCOs. He told us he would keep us briefed on the subject and would inform us before the Germans arrived. We did not altogether agree with this and told him so.

The Sicily landings, which took place on the 10th July 1943, finally extinguished all hope Italy had of winning the war since losing North Africa to the Allies in 1942. This had opened up a war front against Italy from which there was no way out. The Axis had lost North Africa to the Allies opening up a front against Italy.

These military conditions were to be discussed at the 'Gran Consiglio Fascista' on the 24th July where Savo opposed Mussolini. Mussolini was unaware of the conspiracy against him. The King, Vittorio Emanuele III, decided to fire Mussolini in order to save Italy and in particular, its monarchy. Despite the fact that twenty years earlier he had wanted Mussolini to be the Prime Minister.

At 5pm on the 24th July, Mussolini proudly entered the 'Sala del Pappagallo' where the Gran Consiglio Fascista took place. At 3am the next day, the members of the Gran Consiglio Fascista took a vote and came to a decision. Mussolini was no longer Prime Minister on a vote of 19 out of 28. Badoglio was to take over the role. At 5pm, Mussolini went to the Royal Palace to try and convince the King to change his mind but was arrested for his own safety.

Vittorio Emanuele III wanted to completely eradicate fascism from Italy. However the King could reveal his plans as the Italians were still allied to the Germans. For this reason, he only fired Mussolini in a Coup d'Etat.

In spite of this, it was clear (especially to Hitler) that Italy was about to extricate itself out of the war. Hitler decided to start a swift campaign against Italy in order to arrest the King. The non-fascist Italians fearing an imminent German Offensive started fighting with the Allied forces. With the signing of the Armistice on 8th September 1943, Italy's alliance with Germany ended. All the prisoners of war imprisoned in Italy were transferred to prisons in Germany, Ukraine and Poland (eg Auschwitz).

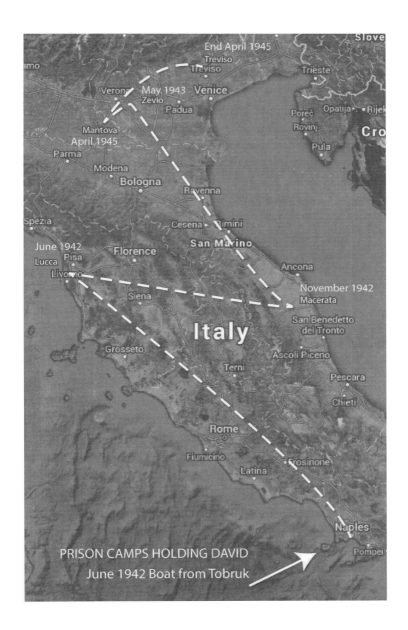

End April 1945
Treviso
Treviso
Verona May 1943 Venice
Zevio
Padua
Mantova
April 1945
Parma
Modena
Bologna
Ravenna
Spezia
Cesena Rimini
San Marino
June 1942
Lucca Pisa
Florence
Livorno
November 1942
Macerata
Siena
San Benedetto
del Tronto
Grosseto
Ascoli Piceno
Italy
Terni
Pescara
Chieti
Rome
Fiumicino
Frosinone
Latina
Naples
PRISON CAMPS HOLDING DAVID
Pompei
June 1942 Boat from Tobruk

CHAPTER 9

ESCAPE PLANS

In July we had a meeting because there was a lot of speculation about Badoglio taking over the Italian army. It was decided that at the end of July we would let one of our platoons (No.1) make their escape. I agreed to the plan. I had been in charge of this platoon but several weeks before the escape I agreed to swap over with Lance Corporal Onions from No.2. He was counted amongst their friends. It gave me a change of scenery and I was able to mix with different men.

Later in the month, it was decided that No.1 platoon would escape the next day on a Monday morning. As the NCO, I was the only one to be briefed about the plan. The men were supposed to be oblivious until the very last moment. However the usual buzz was going around the camp due to one NCO who couldn't keep his mouth shut!

On the Monday morning, No.1 gathered all their gear together as they wouldn't be returning to camp. All the groups going out lined up for a roll call. The Italian officer came out. He was a very nice man had been good to us. Immediately, he called out my name in No.1 but I wasn't there, I was in No.2. "Oh no, you've changed over" he said. Several men had swapped over in the previous weeks, but the Italian Officer insisted that each man return to his respective platoons.

I was now back in charge of No.1 platoon with no instructions on the escape plan, it had been with Corporal Onions the night before. I knew that on the walk to the field, we would 'do the necessary' by disarming the guards and making our escape. I had no spare clothes, no food or anything. I was in the clothes I stood up in - my shorts and shirt. But nothing could be done, we had to move.

We started on a 6 mile trek to a farm that I had never been to before. After a mile or so from camp, we crossed a hill and left the road to trek across the fields. I was told that this would be the best place to un-arm the two guards. To be honest, it was very easy. We took the bullets and the pins out of their rifles and threw them away. We tied the guards up and secured their hands with rope - but not too secure. They asked us what we were doing and why. We told them of our intention to 'escape' and suggested that they abscond too. What they did – we'll never know.

It was a bit strange really because Onions had plans about what he was going to do. But I didn't have any plans at all. I'd been warned about the escape but I didn't know that I was going to be in charge of it until now! However, we went on across the field.

I said "Right, the first thing we've got to do is move back towards camp." "Move back to camp?" came the shocked response of the men. "Oh yes," I said, "We'll move back and stay in the maize grove within 500 yards of the camp and next to the canal." So we doubled back to the big corn field which was flanked by a river on one side and a road on the other.

We lay there waiting. Within a couple of hours, the alarm had been raised that the escape had happened. The camp sent out all kinds of troops looking for us but they passed us by as they were looking further afield.

We stayed there for nearly a week eating the young maize and bits of bread from the Red Cross parcel some of the men had brought with them. We drank water from the canal. One of the group suggested swimming the river to try and locate food. He did this and returned with several bits of food i.e. bread and meat – holding it above his head as he swam. There was a little bit for each person. The following day two men went over and did the same thing.

Camaraderie was good even though the men kept everything for themselves. In fact, one man had a full kit bag but never shared a thing. He still expected everyone else to share with him. After a week, we approached different houses to ask for bits of bread.

CHAPTER 10

STARTING THE LONG TREK

After five or six days, we started to march towards the Adriatic Sea with Venice in mind - heading for the Yugoslavian border. With a small compass and old map, we had some idea of where we were going instead of just marching along. We adopted army patrol tactics by moving during the evening for four hours whilst searching for somewhere to stay all day in the fields. We had two scouts ahead of us. One scout was up front, 50 yards ahead of the other. This worked for about 4 nights until no one wanted to be lead scout. The vacancy had to be filled by me. I think it was at this moment that my whole sense of fear disappeared – someone had to show by example – why not me? I realised that fear was a state of the mind.

At 8 o'clock one evening I was the lead scout when I came across a gate on the lane we were following. It was difficult to open and by this time the rest of the group had caught up with me. We forced open the gate and walked into a big yard where the Germans were refusing vehicles. I gave a casual wave and walked through – the rest following. We were surprised nobody followed. I expect the Germans were wondering who we were.

We found a barn to sleep in. The owner discovered us and said we could stay there, but if the Germans came he wanted us to say that he didn't know that we were there. The Italians were frightened to death of the reprisals carried out by the Germans. All the time we had been living off the land and begging food from some of the Italian peasants. The two of us who could speak a little Italian did all the begging – each time we chanced our arm of being caught whilst the others were hiding out. We were mostly fortunate but occasionally we received nothing, some of the people simply had nothing to spare.

In order to get to the town of Bonavigo, we had to cross a guarded bridge over the river Adige with two Germans at each end. With its banks of thick mud, the river was too wide at 500 yards to swim across plus we had non-swimmers. It was six o'clock in the evening when I decided to take firm action and take the chance to march the men over in double file. I instructed the men "What we'll do is form into groups and we'll march over the bridge unarmed. Respect the German guard and if they stop us, then we stop, fair enough." We did just this and the German guards saluted us in return for my salute. We carried on through the town and when in the countryside we went into the fields to relax. It was so easy but most of the men were scared as hell. That particular night we slept in a copse and waited until the next night before we moved on.

After Bonavigo, we reached the outskirts of Padua one evening at about 8.30pm. We took to our heels when we heard dogs barking with the German soldiers. We raced across a field and reached a stream – too wide for most of the men to jump. 'Lofty' made a bridge of his body over the stream with no hesitation. I held his feet and he fell forward holding a branch and they were able to jump one foot on his back and then over. It was a job pulling him back but I managed it – we jumped and then ran. In all probability, we weren't being chased, but who asks questions at a time like this?

We went into a field and divided ourselves around the field in twos. If one of these groups got captured, the rest of us would still be free. At 5 o'clock in the morning one of the men came to me and said he was unable to waken 4 of the men. Chaos ensued as we pulled them into centre of the field but after a long resuscitation they all started breathing properly. Apparently there was a factory producing sulphur nearby and the waste products were flowing in a steam near them – so it was the sulphur fumes.

We now wanted to avoid the increasingly heavy traffic on the Venice road towards the border. We assumed that the military lorries and troops were moving from Yugoslavia into the Italian front. With such a large group of twelve men, it was decided to split up into smaller units. Six decided to go on their own, two decided to go their own and I was left with the 3 others - **Riches, Reed and Rigden.** They were the ones to come with me - two weaklings and one that wasn't!

I have been very careful not to mention the names of the 12 men. I only know that the 3 with me definitely got back safely - plus one other. I know nothing about the fate of the others even though I heard many rumours. But there was no information I could be certain about.

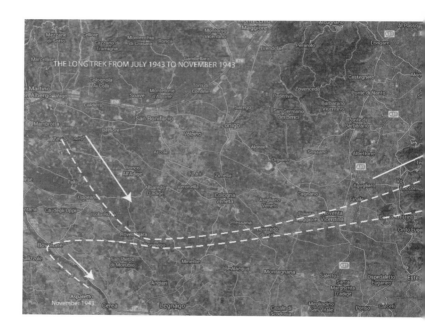

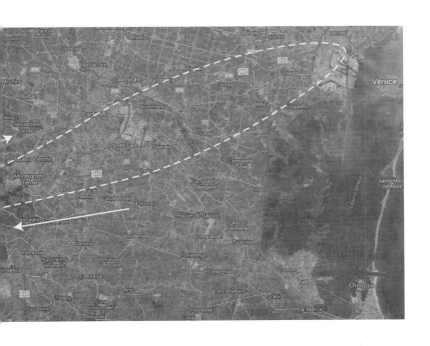

The long trek from July 1943 to November 1943

CHAPTER 11

THE FOUR R's

Our unit of four included Fred Riches from Diss, Les Rigden from Dover and Ernest Reed from Portsmouth who was much older than the rest of us by about 14 years. We decided after a brief talk to return towards the troops in the South - back where we had come from.

After stopping a couple of nights in Padua, we travelled to Bonavigo stopping overnight in a barn. This time I suggested we wait until one o'clock when it was guard change and siesta time. So precisely at one, we went up the bank and walked over. Poor Les Rigden – when we reached cover had to change his pants. We rested in the barn we had used before, relieved at our good fortune. Food for four was easier to come by – I was often asked in for a meal, but had to refuse because of the others. One of the things people asked for was a note from us to say they had helped us.

We had to cross the bridge armed by the Germans again but this time, the set of rules was different. We got to the bridge at midday and as usual the camp guards were there but changing the guard. We slipped under the bridge, over the side, up the side of the bridge, up a bank the side of the bridge and walked across the bridge to the other side. Rigden was in a hell of a state. We stopped up there for a 3 or 4 days in a house and barn recovering from the ordeal. After this we moved down to a place called Bovolone.

After spending the night in a field beside a brick works, we had to cross a main road into a lane opposite. We had just crossed when a German troop carrier came along loaded with soldiers. They shouted to us and we dashed down the lane to a river. We went straight through the river and into the bushes where we lay still for quite a long period. The Germans came down to the river but went off either side so we weren't seen. Eventually we went into a field to dry off our soaking wet clothes.

We saw a man working quite a long way from us but really didn't concern ourselves. About two hours later a lady arrived with a jug of soup which was very gratefully received. We thanked her and went on our way.

The place was Bovolone, full of canals and lakes, it seemed quite a lot safer than most of the places we had been in. There were two huts in a field so we went into those for the night and remained there the following day. A lady called Clara came to us the following evening with food and said we could sleep in her barn. Her husband was terrified and didn't really want to know. The next day she suggested we go further up the valley to a family called Passilongo who had a farm. We could camp on his land.

Bridge at Bovolone

The only road into Bovolone was over a bridge near the town itself. We managed to get into the middle of the place and stayed there for a few days. We got to know some people who kindly gave us soup etc.

It was September and we heard that Italy was out of the war with Badoglio taking over the Italian Army. This was good for us in one sense but bad in another. All the Italian soldiers absconded by leaving their regiments and scattering around Italy. German soldiers were sent out in large numbers to search and round the Italian soldiers up. Warnings were posted up telling the Italians not to help any Italian soldiers or escaped prisoners of war. The consequences if found out, would be death.

This made things more difficult and we could hardly blame the Italians for not helping us.

This meant that we were also in mortal danger from getting caught. We stayed out of sight in the woods and the mountainous part of Italy. Just going out for a bit of food and returning again. We got a lot of help from the Italian people with food such as cooked turkey heads or chicken feet and giblets.

We met the Passilongo family in the middle of the woods, miles from anywhere. They were farmers living in the wilds. I built some small maize huts to sleep in on the side of the fields with the maize cane they supplied. Sig Passilongo had five children and one of his daughters was engaged to an Italian soldier who had absconded and was naturally on the run. He resented us as we were really a threat to him! We stayed there for about a week.

During that week the huts we had previously slept in had been machine-gunned by German planes and set on fire. German patrols then appeared in the area. German officers had been seen rowing up the river in a boat. The family concluded that they were looking for us and this frightened them. Sig Passilongo was worried that if we got caught, his family would be shot. He politely asked us to move on and understanding their feelings we left.

It was now November and progress was very slow. The weather in that area of Italy was especially known for its heavy rainfall in October/November. On a fine day we would attempt to dry out our clothes in a remote area of a field or copse. Many a night was spent with our wet clothes on top only to find that the frost had frozen them. It wasn't pleasant, but at that stage we were beyond caring.

It was early in December when the first snow fell. I met a man living on a hill beside a wood, well away from villages or towns. He shared the whereabouts of the German camp and their A/AC guns but more importantly where they regularly patrolled. (I kept in touch with him for over a year and a half.)

Carrying out his instructions we made our way down to the valley towards Asparetto. On reaching a copse, we saw a stone building nearby in the middle of a field. We used to often sleep in similar huts but for some reason, I didn't fancy this particular one. So we stayed in the woods beside it. The following morning we saw footmarks in the snow where somebody had been searching with dogs. They were big footprints and looked like military ones, looking in the hut and back again. This proved that our previous informant had been right.

Bridge over Adige at Bonavigo

CHAPTER 12

MEETING THE FERRARIS

We stayed in this area as the weather was foul, on the second day at 6pm two young Italians found us and approached. One of them said "Come to my house, my mum doesn't worry about the Germans, I'll take you all for some food". I expressed my concern about the danger of going to their home. He went off on his bicycle returning half an hour later saying we could sleep in his stable.

This young man was called Giovanni Ferrari, the son of Marina with whom we finally stayed with for one and a half years. They had very little food themselves but they gave us what they had - a meal of minestrone and bread. For the first time in years we went to sleep in a warm stable with a feeling of contentment. In the morning, we said we'd move on but they said "No, no, no" as the weather was too bad. "You stay for a little bit longer."

For a couple of days it meant we were able to relax. However I then felt a bout of fever coming over me. I had had this in the desert where it lasted only a couple of days. But at this time – what could I do? I spoke to the other three and decided to walk into the German camp to give myself up. I hoped that I would be able to get some medical treatment there. It was about 10 o'clock in the morning and I had given the others my compass and maps. Marina asked where I was going and

I told her the truth so as to avoid any confusion. She immediately said no and insisted that I stayed. Her son helped me into the house and into bed. I knew nothing for the next five or six hours until I awoke. The fever had broken and I began to sweat. Within two days I was feeling better again, but Marina had been to a doctor. She told him a story about her nephew in Yugoslavia and he let her have a box of phials containing egg injections to inject into me. He said after the war that he guessed she was trying to help someone who was unable to get medical treatment, perhaps an escaped prisoner of war. I was sorry that I couldn't have met him. However, after many attempts the injections were made and I made a quick recovery.

View from Asparetto

The house was situated about a mile from the village. My Italian had improved tremendously and so I learnt that Marina's husband had committed suicide after being called up for the army in 1941. She was left with

Church in Asparetto

three children, Giovanni who had to join the army, Mario who was 17 and 8 year old 'Chico' (or Venario). The 88 year old Nonna (grandmother) and Marina's niece Redorna also lived in the house.

Of the whole family, the only two living up until 1994 are Venario who lived in Vercelli and Redorna who resided in Reggio Melia.

Mario and Marina worked hard to keep the farm going. Having an interest in farming, I decided to earn my keep and offer to help. Whilst the other three men stayed all day in the stable, I was out with the plough or doing whatever was needed – eg hedging, ditching etc. Eventually, the other three were put well out of sight in an old store room with two beds at the top of the house and kept secret there. They joined us every evening in the house for a meal. I was going out to work every day dressed mainly in shorts. I had no other clothes except a pair of trousers but in the warmest weather shorts were the only option.

Farm house in Asparetto

Giovanni had absconded from the army. He disliked agricultural work but had a love of motor bikes. His brother, Mario didn't like it either, but did quite a bit. I found myself doing all the ploughing and planting etc. with Marina and I quite enjoyed it. I got to know the two cows we used for the ploughing.

This left Mario to exploit his own way of life which was buying and selling tobacco on the black market. This proved quite a big money earner and everyone had a hand in it. The expert, of course, was Marina who could take a leaf of tobacco and roll it into a cigar in no time. Giovanni invented a machine with a guillotine which worked by turning a big handle forcing the blade to cut the tobacco about the thickness of 1mm. We built a false wall enclosing the machine. At night we worked by cutting the tobacco. We had two men outside on guard just in case anyone approached. However, the machine when being turned could be heard two hundred yards away.

Another occupation at night was the killing of pigs and calves for friends who did not wish to give half of their meat to the government. I cut most of it up and was given the liver or belly for our work. This helped in the feeding of the whole family. We had so many of these jobs that we had to turn some of them down. The difficulty was it had to be done at night, the Germans imposed a curfew at 9 o'clock and we often encountered German patrols on our way back. One particular night we had to stay put until 5 o'clock in the morning because it wasn't safe to move.

Mario was doing a lot of work such as fishing, working at the market where a lot of bargains are struck with regard to bartering. Having me working the farm gave him more freedom.

Every month the wheat had to be taken to the mill for grinding, the ration was very small so it meant bribing the miller to do extra for us. He would mill the ration first and we would have to give him 50kg of wheat before he would mill 50kg for us. Actually we couldn't afford it, but with clever manipulation by Mario we managed really well. On the following day, we could then bake the bread. The women would mix the dough whilst I put the faggots of wood into the oven outside. These ovens are built about 5ft off the ground about 8ft long with the roof of an oval shape. The door was about 2ft square. Wood was burnt in it until white hot then the ashes removed – wiped with a damp cloth and then the bread inserted with a large wooden pale. When full the door would be closed and sealed with wet clay. About 3 hours later the door would be opened and some bread removed for immediate use – then sealed again and left until the following morning. This bread was very hard called biscotti and was used for breakfast with coffee substituted with the meagre ration from the shop.

Fred Riches had been a baker back home and he helped bake the bread for the family and others in the village.

The Hideout for all things English

ASPARETTO

There were about four families living close by who knew about us – although only two of them knew there were four persons. One house about 200 yards away had a radio and I was allowed to listen to the overseas news on occasions. At that particular time the war news wasn't very exciting.

One man I was introduced to was an antique dealer called Raymondo Merlini, he was quite a wealthy man and said he wished to help us. I met him on many occasions. We travelled away together to meet with the partisan organisation whose main occupation was to blow up railway lines. We had the job of loosening the nuts and bolts on the sleepers. After about 3 months they disbanded and fled to the mountains. I always had a feeling that they were causing terror amongst the local people – confiscating their livestock and money. However, we were too far away to come under suspicion.

Raymondo supplied us with money, fruit, vegetables and flour which helped the whole family. I saw him regularly over the 1 ½ years that I was there. Every evening the other three men would join us for a walk in the fields. It was very difficult for them being cooped up all the time but for their own sakes it was for the best.

I worked as the Italians did with bare feet, and could speak the local dialect very well. I spoke regularly with German soldiers and found a good way of getting food from them. Every day two men would pass our farm with a large trolley containing hay boxes with hot food. We called them into the farm for a glass of wine – putting their trolley behind a wall so that it could not be seen from the road. Marina would take them in for a drink whilst I ladled out enough for 8 of us, and filled it with water – meat stew, goulash, all kinds of meat dishes. This went on until the Germans were replaced by Russian prisoners of war. We invited them in and they offered us the food. We had some very good meals especially as meat had been off our ration for about 2 years.

BARN FIRE

In one of the fields we had dug out a cave from a hedge with a ditch running alongside. Anything English was kept in there – safer than in the building. During the hot weather – siesta time was 1.00pm until 4.00pm when everything went quiet, Ernest Reed often joined me in the yard for a talk One day the German Ack Ack were firing on an American bomber and our barn caught on fire. We put the fire out but the barn was ruined – however the Germans paid up. They believed the story, but Ernest and I knew different!!

USING EVERYTHING

The house we lived in had two bedrooms at the front and at the rear upstairs two store rooms which were converted bedrooms for my colleagues. The dining room had a large fireplace and a wood-burning stove. There was no electric, gas or oil for lamps. Our only source of light was candles, which were homemade. Water was drawn from a pump outside and at the back was a well from which you drew water either for yourself or for the animals.

When a pig was killed, everything was used – the lard was used to conserve the meat – the skin and bones emulsified to produce soap. The amount of rations the Italian families were allowed was small, bordering on nil. You couldn't get things like salt, pepper, soap, paraffin, sugar, butter or margarine, even olive oil was rationed. We made our own molasses from sugar beet which served as a sweetener. Butter was made every day; the milk from the morning milking was left standing all day then the cream taken off, put into a bottle and shaken for about an hour until the butter formed – everyone took their turn in shaking – then the butter was taken out and used for cooking. In the morning the overnight milk was separated and the same procedure took place all over again.

For washing clothes the ashes from the wood are sieved then put into boiling water – instant washing powder. The sheets on the beds were changed every week – the soiled ones put into a big wardrobe. In May and October, the women of all the families – around 20 women go to the river and the sheets – about 60 from our house are taken by cow and cart to the river for washing. I used to take them down there at 9 o'clock and at 5 o'clock collect them all dry and folded ready to pack away. The next day someone else would have theirs done – and so on until all completed. Apparently a full linen cupboard was part of a bride's inheritance.

The same system was used in the crops – whether it was wheat, barley, potatoes or corn, each farmer helped the other. I quite enjoyed going to the other farms as it gave you an insight into other Italian homes and their methods.

TOBACCO TRADE

Every week people would arrive either from Milan or Turin for cut tobacco. One particular couple stick in my memory – a man with a hunched back about the age of 50 and a young lady of about 20. She put cut tobacco in all parts of her clothing – even in the straps of her bra – top of stockings – really got loaded. Every time they said the man was stopped and searched. Naturally he never carried any and she just waltzed through – once she had over 20lb of cut tobacco concealed on her, which meant a lot of money for us and a big profit for them.

LUCKY ESCAPE

Every Sunday afternoon there was a film show in Cerea about 4 miles away – the boys tried to encourage me to go with them, but I wasn't willing to take a chance just to see a film. Then it happened – the film started at 3.30 and at 3.45 the Germans surrounded the place and took away all the people without papers. Giovanni was once again lucky – he arrived late. About 30 young men were arrested and sent to Germany in labour camps (at least that is what we were told). As much as I would have liked to let the other 3 men have more liberty I thought it best they stay under cover most of the time. If they were in the house on Sundays we always kept a look-out in case someone approached – the dog was a great help – no one could come into the back of the farm with him there.

It was pretty obvious to me that the Germans were trying to conserve fuel – they commandeered oxen from some of the farms and were using them to take ammunition to the A/A guns and for moving heavy machinery. The oxen are very strong, but it is a slow process.

AMERICAN DROP IN

One afternoon in May, 1944 there was a daylight raid by American bombers over Verona – one plane was hit and the crew bailed out. We saw one come down into a marsh – Mario and I ran over and were the first to reach him. What a surprise when I spoke to him in English. Mario rolled up the parachute and as the Germans approached I told him to hide under a small bridge. We knew some of the Germans and pointed them in a false direction as to where he had gone. Ten minutes afterwards when it was all clear he came out, and refused help from us saying he had to make his way to a certain rendezvous. We wished him well – he thanked us and we accompanied him a short way and put him on the right track. That parachute came in very handy – not a bit of it was wasted.

D DAY

On June 5th I went to Remo to listen to the news at 9 o'clock – there was nothing unusual about it. The following morning at 8 o'clock one of the girls 14 years old came over and asked me to listen to the BBC as something had happened but they couldn't quite get the gist of it. First of all we listened to the Italian broadcast which said of an attempted landing which had been repulsed and left thousands of British and American dead on the beach. At 9 o'clock the Overseas Broadcast gave a different story about the D Day landing. I listened intently for most of the day and was able to give the news as it came through. At 6 o'clock pm the German and Italian radio stations declared the news was false.

The following day even the newspapers had the headlines – 'Invasion in Normandy Repulsed'. It caused quite a bit of confusion – the four of us knew what to believe – but it was very difficult to convince the Italians. It took about 4 days for the papers to admit to the invasion. Of course we were elated, but still had to compose ourselves – there was quite a long way go yet.

We were hay-harvesting at the time and I can remember the raids over Northern Italy becoming more frequent. Some of the planes dropped leaflets and many found their way into our hands.

CHAPTER 13

WORKING ON THE FARM

Marina had a sister who lived in Trieste and another relation who lived in Udine. They came to us on a couple of occasions to get food to take back. It just proved to me that practically the whole of Italy was short of food. Of course they were so close to Yugoslavia and that made a big difference. The partisans made many a raid on their food supplies. It was the basic food they took back with them, flour – salt (if we had any) tomato puree – which we had plenty of as we made our own, onions (precious things) and some of our own produce of coffee beans. They went back loaded – I know they used the train but wondered how they got to the station as it was at least 10 miles away, and there was no such thing as public transport. All the time I was there I never saw a civilian car or motor bike. The few motorised vehicles were all German.

WINE PRODUCING

August and September were very busy months with the harvesting of wheat and corn – then comes the wine season. Marina each day checked the vines and then we would start on wine making. A big wooden box with lathes across the bottom was put over a large tray. The name sounds like a "swall" it is of course for the treading of grapes – we had 2 types of grapes to pick

The four R's taken at the farm summer 1944

Top left – David, Top right – Ernest, Bottom left – Les, Bottom right – Fred with Tanike the dog

with cow and cart. I would bring in the grapes and the other English boys were taking it in turns treading – very tiring work. All the juice plus skins and pips we put into open vats. One must be careful that no leaves are included. It will stay like this for about 4 days and then it is drawn off and put into barrels.

The taste of the wine for two days is very nice but gradually it tastes bitter and one has to wait for it to mature for at least 4 months.

The skins, pips and pulp were then distilled – illegal of course but necessary. Giovanni made the still – he welded the lid of a saucepan after filling it with the pulp – a tube fitted through the lid reaching about 6' high then coiled down through a big can of water and into a container. Candles we used for heat and it was a very slow process but the liqueur called Grappa was really strong – it was used in the winter to fortify the coffee on a cold day. One drop of that and you completely forgot the cold. Of course most of the vine growing farms did the same. The wine still had to be decanted again until it was corked. It was very heavy work.

NIGHT FISHING

When food was scarce, Giovanni and I would go night fishing. We took lanterns and some sacks plus a fishing net.

We would go to a small lake about 2 kilometres from the house.

Giovanni would climb up a pylon and bring down the live cable and put it in the lake. The result was that at least 20 fish would be stunned to the surface. We would wade out and collect them and put them into the sacks.

We could see in the distance the lights of a German Motor Cyclist who had been sent out to investigate the loss in power. On reflection it was a pretty dangerous thing to do.

Marina would salt the fish and put the surplus in our underground freezer, which was two metres below ground and packed with solid ice.

ALARM RAISED

An Italian friend came shouting to the house that they were coming! Marina reacted quickly and asked me to get several white sheets and meet her by the grape vines.

I rushed out with the sheets and we hurriedly put the sheets over the first row of vines. Just as we finished we saw it! A swarm of locusts like a massive black cloud approaching the vines. The locusts went over the sheets and the vines were saved. What a thrilling and scary sight it was.

SILK MAKING

From heavy to light work – in November the silkworm cocoons were boiled and the silk stretched across wires in the sun to dry. When it was dry the silk was spun into balls and then woven into cloth. The natural colour is golden but natural dyes are used to change the colour. We had about 6 mulberry trees and during the summer the silkworms were very active – I didn't have a lot to do with them but saw Marina with the chrysalis. She would gather them in a bucket then in November or December and make the silk.

COLDER WEATHER

The winter months meant hard work hedging and ditching – if the weather was bad, all the implements would be cleaned and sharpened plus the fact that the manure heaps had to be moved to the respective fields ready for spreading. At least it was a warm job on a cold day.

It rather surprised me at the amount of snow that fell during January – we were about 30 miles south of

Verona and it was normal to wake up to 6' of snow. The pump was usually frozen but water could always be obtained from the well. If possible I would draw enough water for the animals at night to save cutting through the snow in the morning. One of the good things was that the roads were impassable so the Germans couldn't get through.

METAL COLLECTION

The Germans had been going to houses confiscating metal or machinery. Giovanni had a lathe – it was about 10' long and very heavy – we dug a hole a good 8' deep and with a lot of hard work managed to put the lathe into the hole and after covering it with sand and soil completely covered it with loose straw over the top – at least it would have taken a lot of finding.

We also had 3 rifles and ammunition buried as well – just in case they were needed.

WAR NEWS

The war news was mixed – naturally the break-through by the Germans in Belgium was big news for the papers and once again it does not do anything for the morale. The BBC news revealed the truth that the breakthrough had been stopped – the Italians were quite ready to accept our news as correct now.

THREATS

The Germans executed many Italians who helped allied prisoners and burnt their houses to the ground.

Example of German notice

ANNOUNCEMENT N.6

Pasquato Renato from S. Pietro (Bragadina)

Has been condemned to death penalty and shot.

For a long time he has put up 5 English soldiers.

Furthermore he has had relationships with a chief and a band of insurgents.

His house has been burnt and his family have been arrested.

This announcement is a warning and a call to all the honest people to collaborate.

You are asked to immediately report to this Command all those unknown and suspect people who are on your property or in the villages nearby.

Through this you can protect yourselves and your assets.

The German High Command Legnagno 1944

CHAPTER 14

MAJOR SET BACK

It was on the 5th April, 1944 that I received my biggest reversal. It was two o'clock in the afternoon – Mario came up to me and said he saw Luigi (Les Rigden) go into the barn and get a rifle and ammunition. I went out to see what was happening – he was in one of the fields holding the rifle. Apparently through one of the bedroom windows he saw a line of fascists walking across a field searching for something. Instead of telling me – he decided to take things into his own hands.

He was very distressed and I took the rifle away from him and ushered him to a corner in which we were concealed, but could see the fascists through the fence. He was in quite a state and I was beginning to wonder if I could keep him quiet.

One of the men came through the farm and advanced towards us. I told Les to crawl up the ditch – of course he ran bolt upright.

The fascist actually was only going to relieve himself but turned when he heard someone running. He shouted and the rest of the group came through. They surrounded Rigden and asked him questions – I came up with them, but kept to one side. Not understanding one word they said to him – he turned to me and said "what shall I say to them".

That was it – they turned their revolvers and rifles on me and questioned me – I admitted to being English and we were escorted to Cerea and put into cells – next to one another.

Thoughts immediately turned to escape – the walls were very thick so the only way out was perhaps by the roof. I turned the wooden frame of the bed one its end and tested the ceiling. I was about to dig a hole and at the same time look through an iron barred window into the next cell which contained Les Rigden. I told him of my intention and he begged me not to leave him.

At 7 o'clock in the evening the guards came for us. We were handed over to two plain-clothed SS officials – this puzzled me at the time – why should they worry about two ordinary POWs?. On entering the prison we were strip searched and everything was taken from us. Les Rigden was in a separate room, but I never even thought that he had anything on him that could cause alarm.

How wrong I was, we were put into a big black car. One of the men was brandishing a revolver sat next to me and the other one drove the car.

At about 10 o'clock that night there was a terrific air raid over and around Verona – the car was pulled into the side of the road near a copse – we there nearly two hours. During that time my thoughts were on escape. I asked Les Rigden to attack the driver if I tried to take the one with the gun, he flatly refused to move. I had to give up the idea, tackling one was one thing but with 2 it was pure suicide – no more than I expected from Mr Rigden, he was the cause of us being there, yet was unwilling to co-operate. More was to follow later.

MEETING THE GESTAPO

It was in the early hours of the morning that we arrived at the Gestapo HQ in Verona – at the time I didn't know it was Verona, but found that out later. Then to the first floor into a very large room which contained about 10 SS officers sitting around the walls in armchairs. I was put into the middle of the room and was told to answer their questions in German.

My immediate reaction was "I can't speak the language" and retorted this to them in Italian. For the next two hours the questions came mostly in Italian with a sneaky German remark would I like coffee or some food. Although I did know enough German to understand that, I refused to answer. Les Rigden stood there saying nothing.

CALLED A SPY

Then came the accusation that I was a spy and they had the evidence to prove it. I had nothing on me to relate to that charge and told them so. One of the officers went out of the room and came in with a tray full of paper – of different sizes – immediately I said it wasn't mine and I had never seen them before.

They all belonged to Les Rigden, his pockets must have been stuffed full of all the propaganda leaflets dropped by the Allies – in different languages. Of course he said in English they were being used as toilet paper. They asked me to interpret what he had said in Italian, which I did – they took no notice whatsoever.

The questioning was then about where we had stayed over the previous months.

My answer had to be worded carefully as I did not want to divulge the house of Marina at Asperetto I said we had moved from place to place living off the land – of course they didn't believe me.

It must have been between 4 and 5 o'clock in the morning the two guards came in and took us down to the cells. The same one we had been in like a lion's cage – bars all the way around as well as the top, wooden bunks – that was all.

About an hour later there must have been about 20 women herded out of cells to a row of washbasins for washing. They were given about 5 minutes, then, were sent back to their cells. Next about 20 men were brought out for the same reason. We of course were the subject of curiosity, but none had the chance to speak to us or vice versa.

MORE INTERROGATION

About an hour later the guards came back for just me —
Rigden was left lying on the bed. Back to the same
room, the officers were different, but the same line of
questioning, all the answers were still the same.

Then one of the apparently the one in charge said "You
will be shot as you are wearing civilian clothes. I was
able to tell him — all the clothes I was wearing were
issued either by the British Army or in a POW camp.
The trousers I had on were from the Italian Army, but
had been dyed black.

I told him they had patches on the trousers in prison
camp and on taking them off (the patches) the colour
was different so with the help of some berries I let
them soak they turned black. Actually they had been
dyed with black-berries. I was told to take off my shirt,
trousers and socks — I did so and they were taken away.
About 2 hours later they were returned and the officer
indicated I had told the truth!

It must have been mid-day when I was returned to the
cells — this was a long cell in which there were 17
Italians and Les Ridgen. I was given the first food for
about 24 hours.

The Italians quickly pointed that it was the condemned
cell and they were all awaiting execution. Most of them

were in there for either hiding or feeding enemies of the Germans. Some were in there for other reasons.

For the next three days I went through interrogation and then on the fourth day, I thought I have got nothing to lose and answered every question in English. Not one of them understood and when I was prompted to speak Italian I still spoke only English.

The following day the same thing, I was told I would get no food unless I co-operated – for this I retorted in Italian, this was no hardship I had been starving many times. Back to the cells again.

EXECUTION

It was a very grim moment the first two had been taken out that morning for execution and there was stillness amongst the men there. There was one guard – Italian and a fascist who was about the worst one we had come in contact with – he always came in and with a rifle and bayonet and prodded the one he wanted.

At that moment I was feeling bitter having to endure interrogation daily whilst Les Rigden who caused all the trouble sat back and waited – often the so called meal was cold when I returned and I vent my feelings on this guard, strange to relate – he backed off and went out of the cell.

The following morning he came into the cell and called me outside – everyone expected the worst. However, outside in the corridor he said that an English Officer had been brought in during the night and would I like to speak with him? I nodded a yes and returned to my cell – I wasn't taken for questioning that day and at about noon he called me out again and took me to a cell containing a Captain Evans.

This Captain said he had been captured whilst fighting with the partisans – we exchanged a few words and I was taken back. Strange to relate this Italian guard was so different to us all after that.

CHAPTER 15

MEETING THE DOCTOR

On about the eighth day German guards came for me, but this time I had to go up two flights of stairs and had to wait outside an office door. After a short time there I was marched into the office and sitting at a desk was a small man with rimless spectacles and wearing a long white coat. I thought I recognised him but put it to the back of my mind.

I remember his first question so clearly – "so you refuse to co-operate with the German Officers?" I replied "no I refuse to speak in any other language other than my own – which is English" His next question was "What part of England do you come from?" I replied "Torquay". He said "I lived in Torquay for six years".

Of course – I said I thought I recognised you. He went on asking me where I lived and worked, the name of my shop manager, and then I remembered, we delivered meat to his house. He smiled and told the guards to leave the room. He asked me to sit on a chair beside him and ordered coffee. He said he was a Doctor at Devonport Dockyard, his name was Muller.

I was talking to him for about two hours and asked him when and why he returned to Germany – he said it was in 1938 when his country needed him – no other argument.

He asked me how Torquay had fared during the bombing and I had to reply that I didn't know – I left England in 1940 and had had no communication other than letters to POW camps since, whether this was a catch-question I don't know. Eventually he said I cannot set you free but will see that you are sent to a POW camp. I thanked him and left with a pocket full of biscuits.

SORROW

Two days later Ridgen and I were called out and taken to an Army HQ to transport to a prison camp.

I must point out that only seven of the inmates were left in that cell – the others had perished – I felt sorry to think they were helping us only to be condemned in this way.

To reflect on my treatment from the Gestapo, I must say the questioning was tough and each time I seemed to be in there for hours, but I had no violence shown against me. The one thing I had to protect was Marina's family and no way would I have divulged that. It was just as well that only I was interrogated.

MOVE TO MANTOVA

That afternoon we were taken by lorry to a security prison at Mantova. The camp was not very large – in two sections UK and American – the other for Poles, Hungarians, Russians and Gurkhas.

On entering the camp I was interviewed by an American Officer who was the man in charge. As soon as he knew I could speak Italian and knew quite a bit about Verona and the surroundings he asked me to join the escape committee – this I did and became familiar with the workings of the camp immediately.

There was a high wall on the side of the camp – I learned later that the River Po was the other side.

Several escapes were in the pipeline – only one made it, days later he came back in under guard. Not knowing the language was his downfall.

Les Rigden came up to me one day and said he had spoken to an American who had just entered the camp with another man.

He asked "Where are the toilets"!? Strange request from a POW, as we used other words for them. I reported to the Sergeant, who called both men to a committee meeting.

After being given their place of birth and GI numbers and unit, the Sergeant immediately said you are spies, then, proceeded to ask them if they were German. They denied this, although we could detect they were telling lies.

We asked what took place and we were told, how the state of a person was or came from tied up with the GI number – plus the unit mentioned was still in America.

They were recalled and so they stayed in the camp and were locked up for the night, but did not walk out in the morning.

Quite a serious threat, but it paid dividends – at the six o'clock roll call, these two men were removed from the camp by the Germans. The Poles told us they would have used different methods.

CHAPTER 16

GUNFIRE

We could hear heavy gunfire in the distance but it seemed so far it did not do a lot for our morale, but one morning at roll call the Germans seemed to be in a panic – we were told to get our belongings and put into groups of about 20 men – in our group were 3 Frenchmen, one a Captain – 3 Ghurkhas, 10 Americans and 4 English.

We were put on a coach with 7 guards – one with a machine gun mounted on the roof. There four coaches in the convoy and we headed north. An escape plan was put into operation using pepper in blankets to overpower guards but the opportunity to carry it out didn't materialise – we also had an escort of motor cycles and side cars. We reached Treviso and stayed the night, then up to the Brenner Pass in an isolated place – a big building very bare – cold – damp and once again we had to sleep on the floor.

The weather was atrocious – snow fell very heavily and two mornings we were unable to get out until 11 o'clock. Luckily we were only there a few days and then heard the rumbling of gunfire.

It was on May 3rd that we were locked in for the night and we thought we heard German vehicles leaving the camp. At daybreak a Ghurkha climbed up to look out of the window (which was about 20' from the ground) and he reported the Germans had gone – no guards or anything.

We had quite a job to force the doors and in the distance could see tanks approaching firing their guns and the Germans retaliating.

AMERICANS ARRIVE

About three hours later the Americans arrived – what a relief – the feeling after nearly three years cannot be described. It wasn't very long before we were taken in vehicles to a base point – then into lorries loaded with American casualties – walking wounded!!

LIBERTY AT LAST

Back through Northern Italy to Treviso. There had been a battle there the day before and it was not very nice to encounter what devastation can be caused. Then on to Verona where we stopped for 2 hours before driving to Bologna. The Americans gave us K. Rations – good for them but the amount of protein they contained didn't do our stomachs any good – we hadn't been used to it.

On May 8th, 1945 we arrived in Florence, and the end of war in Europe was announced. There was a general sigh of relief but when I saw the long columns of German prisoners of war, dishevelled, unhappy and everything else which we suffered – I felt very sorry for them – perhaps they received better treatment than we did – nevertheless the stigma is still there.

FLIGHT TO BARI

In the afternoon a DC7 flew us to Bari when we had to go through a medical and the full dose of inoculation plus the usual system of delousing etc.

It is rather an embarrassing situation as the majority of men didn't really need it. The counselling by WVS officials was to be a waste of time, they were unable to tell us of any personal information, only general information which was of little interest to us at that time.

The amount of money paid to me was in my mind miserable to say the least. The last pay I had received was in March, 1942 and to pay out £1.10 per person was disgraceful.

After buying toilet requisites from the NAAFI, it left me with the princely sum of 10/-. One telegram was allowed per person – I sent mine to Torquay which – I found out later caused quite a bit of confusion – the reason – I left Barry in 1940 and the telegram spelt Bari incorrectly!

NAPLES AND HOME

The following day we boarded a train for Naples —
spent one night there in a transit camp and on the 15th
May boarded a Norwegian ship bound for England.

The next day we went by train to Haywards Heath in
Sussex. There, after two days of refitting out, were
interrogated and then allowed to relax before being
given leave tickets and warrants to go home.

CHAPTER 17

PATRICIA'S WAR

My parents got engaged in early 1939 and only met up once more that year after the outbreak of war.

My mother was a civil servant who was evacuated to Blackpool from London in 1940. She joined the WRAC in 1943 with her friend Elsie. Patricia was a Private but as an established civil servant she received a Captain's salary. My mother had joined up after my Dad had gone missing in the war, presumed dead. His photo was in the 'Torquay Times' and this gave her strong the motivation to directly join in the war effort. She was given a specialist role after completing her training at Bicester and she took lodgings run by a Miss Fowler in Vicarage Road, Birmingham.

Her appointment was to a Personal Assistant to Lady Reading, who was a Jewish aristocrat.

Patricia in 1943

Lady Reading was a woman with great influence and she was the co-founder of the Women's Voluntary Service in 1938 and was appointed by Churchill to organise a network of crèches throughout the industrial areas so that mothers could still work in the munitions factories. She was made a DBE in 1941 and promoted to Dame Grand Cross in 1944, then in 1955 she became a Life Peer and was the first woman to take her seat in the House of Lords.

Lady Reading

It was Patricia's job between 1943 and 1945 to co-ordinate her appointments and meetings and whilst she admitted to me that Lady Reading was not easy to work for her powers of persuasion were such that you would do whatever she wanted.

Mother went on to tell me that Lady Reading had given her a rectangular wooden box on first starting her role, but she had been instructed never to open it unless the Germans invaded us. After 3 weeks, she could resist no more so opened up the box. Inside was a travel pass which had been signed and authorized by Winston Churchill. It gave the order that Lady Reading could commandeer any form of transport to get to Manchester Airport as quickly as possible. The implication being that she could be flown to the USA, as she would have been in mortal danger had the Nazis invaded and conquered England.

My mother was convinced that my father David was still alive but had to wait until 1945 to find out!

They got married in Southall, London where my mother was brought up. Then, when Dad was de-mobbed they set up home in St.Marychurch, Torquay. Once we had started school, Mum joined the Red Cross and worked with them on a voluntary basis for 28 years.

CHAPTER 18

MARINA LEARDINI (Ferrari)

Marina was born in Trieste in 1898. She married at about 18 and moved to Asparetto in 1930. She had three sons called Giovanni, Mario and Venario when the English P.OW's arrived at the farm in November 1943.

Marina had sadly lost her husband in 1941 and managed the farm largely on her own. It was on the edge of Asparetto, with a barn, two cows and a couple of hectares of land. The land is mainly flat with water ditches for irrigation.

One of the good things Mussolini did was to introduce effective irrigation!

The fact that Marina gave shelter to four POW's when it was freezing outside was an act of humanity and kindness. The fact that she let them stay for over eighteen months is a remarkable example of generosity and selflessness. The risk to her life and that of her children was real and everyday could be your last. The Germans were all around Asparetto and often visited the farm. Marina's resourceful way of feeding eight people was just incredible.

She had numerous skills, from Tobacco cutting and rolling cigars to making use of any resource available.

She could have written a manual on "100 Ways to Use A Pig." She was a true heroine.

My father had real love, admiration and affection for Marina. She was an unsung heroine who made a real difference. She was supported by her niece Redorna, who lived with them, and was born in 1913 so was about 30 when the British arrived.

Marina moved to Vercelli in 1963 and died in 1984. Evidence suggested she had a romantic liaison with one of the escapees (Fred Riches from Norfolk), as letters sent to him by my father hinted at this. Sadly, Redorna never married but kept in touch with my father from time to time.

The legacy of Marina's sacrifice and kindness will live on as we recount the true impact her actions had on us and gave her a special place in all of our hearts. We salute this incredible lady and the lovely people of the Leardini family as well as other Italian friends from Asparetto.

Marina Leardini

Redorna Leardini

CHAPTER 19

RETURNING FROM WAR

After a de-briefing in Bari, my father travelled to Naples where he boarded a Norwegian ship to finally come home. He arrived in Glasgow early in June 1945 and made his way down to Southall to meet my mother Patricia again at last! They were already engaged and decided to marry on my mother's 26th birthday on 29th September 1945.

On his return to Devon, my father discovered that all the wages he had accrued whilst being away had been spent by his mother and family.

He was furious that money had been deducted from his pay and sent to the German government for "looking after" him when he was a prisoner of war. This "looking after" had been very questionable, added to the fact that he was out of their custody from July '43 to April 45. He took this matter up with Herbert Morrison MP, who said that he was sympathetic but the country was bankrupt after the war.

My father approached the government to get some compensation payment for Marina and her family.

The results of his efforts are recorded in the translated letter sent in December 1945.

Asparetto

26/12/1945

Dear Fred (Rosso)

I came back here to the house on the 9th December to find everyone well. In this week, we received your letter and I am so pleased to hear you got married to Catherine, as now I believe you will be happy.

The British Government paid Aunty Marina 40,000 lira, also Memo 40.000, Clera 10,000, Passilongo 8,000 and Errino they gave 1500, only to me they gave nothing.

The British Government itself gave very little to the others?

Write to me with your home address so I can reply, I have written two other letters and hope you will receive them.

I haven't got any news to give you from this house, because aunty said she will write to you to tell you her news.

I send you many regards and wishes for you and to your Catherine to always be happy.

With affection as always

Do you remember Christmas 1944? How much laughter we had with Les?

Redorna Leardini

My parents had hoped to buy a house but all they could afford was to get married and buy some furniture for a rented house in St. Marychurch, Torquay. Raymond was born in July 1946 and Colin and I (twins) in February 1950. My parents were finally able to buy a house in 1958 and it had a bathroom and indoor flushing toilet which was sheer luxury for my mother.

We were lucky enough to live close to the beaches and about 20 minutes way from Dartmoor, so we made regular trips up there and would find bomb craters to shelter from the wind. Trying to find a flat area to play cricket on was quite a challenge.

Dad had constructed a picnic box, which included the vital components of a small primus stove and a kettle to make tea. Money was always tight so I can never remember eating out until we were 12. I had my first train journey at 9 and had my first haircut outside of home at 16.

Dad returned to his job at the Torquay Co-operative Society in late 1945 and became a Branch Manager in 1948. He was still playing football then, every Wednesday in the season, He played on his afternoon off for the local Co-op side.

He started studying by correspondence courses with Loughborough College. He would get up at 4 am to study before he went to work at 6.30am.

He passed his Departmental Exams and then entered a number of academic competitions organised by the Co-operative College in 1959. He won an accountancy competition and his prize was a three week study tour to any European Country. He chose Italy and went there in 1960.

He had been helping to run Co-op Youth Groups and when the Scout Leader at Babbacombe Sea Scouts was taken ill and died, he agreed to take over for a short period, this lasted for four years.

His approach to Scouting was very progressive; he resisted wearing a uniform until he was given no choice. He believed in the team ethic where every scout played a part. So when we were training for scout sports day, every scout had his key task.

The non-athletes all had tasks as time keepers, kit allocation and making sure each competitor was ready. He even allocated a cheer leader.

He insisted that all sea scouts should swim and organised swimming coaching at the close by Palace Hotel.

The Troop became so popular that the scout hut became too small and meetings had to be organised on two evenings each week.

Before the end of each meeting they had a quiet ten minute period when someone told a story.

David told a story about being captured by the Germans. There were 40 boys completely spellbound by this and he was forced to tell other stories about the war by popular demand.

In fact he wrote a paper for Unesco about engaging young people and they were so impressed he was invited in 63 to visit Denmark and Sweden on a study tour to review other countries approach to the subject. He had problems convincing the Co-op that this trip was worthy of their support.

He was subsequently invited to assist Unesco to develop a new policy on youth. However, this was impossible without his employers support.

David had become the Deputy Area Manager in 1962 and Area Manager in 1968.

Robillard family photo taken at Petitor Torquay circa 1953 with Uncle Les on the right my mother's brother

WAR MEDALS

My father never applied for any of these as he felt that war should be avoided at all costs and to parade them on lapels of badges was immodest.

He thought that the state should provide for all the disabled whether they were in the forces or not.

However as his diamond wedding anniversary approached, I managed to persuade him to let me apply for them. I did this in April 2005 and after three months I approached the war medals department. They told me that as ours was a late application it would take some time.

In order to try another avenue, I wrote to Tony Blair the then Prime Minister and asked him to try and arrange an early release of the medals. Mr Blair responded in a few days and the medals were delivered to my office the following week.

The family were very grateful for this and we agreed to the condition that we would not seek to publicise this gesture.

On the 29th September, 2005 David's 60th wedding anniversary my dad wore his medals for just an hour. He then put them back in the boxes. We never spoke about them again, we did manage one photo of him wearing them, albeit a reluctant one!

David and Patricia in the Charente taken 2005

CHAPTER 20

THE END IN THE CHARENTE

Father enjoyed watching sport, especially rugby and cricket. He generally had a team to support in the rugby, as he had France, England and Italy as his favourites.

He had become poorly in 2006, but was stoic despite his condition.

Colin had been very dedicated in helping to nurse our dad and we were grateful that mum had hearing problems, especially in the last week. Dad sadly passed away on 18th February 2007, aged 88.

We arranged the funeral for the following Friday in the church of the local village Salles Lavalette. We managed to find a Protestant minister who conducted the service. It was nice that some French friends came from the village and we produced an obituary about his life in French and English.

It was an especially sad period, as my father-in-law, Jim had died in early January that year and then we had a massive shock when his wife, Sybil passed away the day after my father.

Dad had purchased a plot in the local cemetery in 1994, in Salles Lavalettes. This is where he now rests, under the warmth of the Charente sunshine.

After his passing, my mother was reluctant to come back to England, but is still with us at the grand age of 96. Like Dad, she also loved the Charente but found it hard to cope with summer temperatures in excess of 30 degrees Celsius.

We called their home "Paradise", as it was at the top of a 300m drive, with beautiful views and fields on each side and numerous fruit trees, including fig, cherry, mirabel, apple and plum cherry. Quite often, the stunning view of the 2 Acre field of sunflowers could be seen at the back of the house.

Mother has survived so long by avoiding the excesses of life. She did not like anything loud or late nights and preferred order, flowers and time with family. In contrast, my father could be loud, excitable and at times impolite, but always interesting! He was always objective, and able to promote a discussion on a wide range of subjects. He was a working class intellectual who always made the best of any situation.

David spraying his vines

CHAPTER 21

THAT PLACE CALLED ITALY

I realised from about the age of seven that my dad liked this place called Italy (whatever that was) a lot!

On Mondays, after the Sunday roast, we were given the task of hand mincing the leftover beef. From this, we would have Spaghetti Bolognese, which we loved and would call it our "Italian night".

We were told that our father had been in the war, in the desert and that then he had gone to Italy, where the people were really nice to him.

THE SECRET

My twin brother Colin and I played with the other boys in the road.

We had a terraced house with no bathroom and an outside toilet! We had little to boast about until one day we saw our father putting something away in the cupboard under the stairs. He told us to "go away" but the next morning I dared myself to have a look in this cupboard as dad had gone to work hours before. My eyes nearly popped out of my head when I saw a rack in there with six rifles and actual real bullets in boxes underneath.

What a discovery! Even my brother Colin was impressed, so when other boys were telling us about their brother's penknife or his Dawe's Emblem bike, we would say "oh really? Come and see what we've got!"

We sneaked them into the house and slowly but quietly, would open the cupboard door and watch with delight as their expressions turned to amazement, as they marvelled at the showpiece!

We had connected these rifles with war and somehow this Italy place kept being talked about. I was about 9 when I helped my father deliver some meat to some Torquay restaurants. At one particular place, he used to have a conversation in a completely different language!

Firing rage at Rippon Tor on Dartmoor

CHAPTER 22

TRIP TO ITALY

When we were 10, our father, mother and older brother Raymond went on a trip to Italy. They were going in the new Zephyr, belonging to Uncle Les who was the younger brother of my mother. We loved him, as he once drove over Salisbury Plain at 100mph, with us shouting encouragement from the back to "take him over!" the whole way.

His fiancée was the lovely Aunt Mary, who took Colin and me to Northern Ireland on holiday. We flew from Bristol to Belfast and I nearly choked on a Barley Sugar as I was so excited. We remember Londonderry and Portrush and how cheap Eire was (an ice cream was nearly half the price!). We asked why the police station has sand bags around it, and we were told it was just in case the river flooded, yet only the day before, we had walked to the river and it was 20 minutes away!

It turned out my father had won academic competition with the Co-operative College and the prize was to go to a country in Europe. Dad chose Italy and they drove the whole way to Northern Italy. They were given tours of the Co-operative farms and vineyards in the Po Valley and treated to some amazing meals whilst Uncle Les survived on Frittata (omelette) and patate fritte! (chips).

They also visited Asperetto, where we were told, they had met the wonderful Marina and met friends of hers in the village.

MAKING SALAMI

I remember that they had visited Venice and mother brought back a plastic gondola that lit up and some tea towels! Father was very happy with his 5 litre can of Olio (olive oil) and loads of small white onions (garlic). Evidently he made several salami with cured pork and the local Greeks and Italians would turn up to his butchers shop for a taste!

We lived in St Marychurch then, which was its own town then and had a Baroque town hall. It later became part of Torquay, it bordered the sea and we had so many beaches and caves to explore!

After my parents had visited Italy in 1960, they seemed to receive letters and cards from there on a regular basis. It was quite exciting seeing a letter arrive with a foreign stamp on it, such simple pleasures.

BOMBED

We knew about the war from a young age, the school we would have attended was bombed in 1944 and sadly 21 local children attending Sunday school were killed. The Germans had been bombing the RAF hospital which had been set up at the Palace Hotel in

Babbacombe. Evidently, the large red cross made it a sitting target. As a result, we had to walk to Westhill School, which was quite a trek when you were 4!

We visited Dartmoor quite often and father would go target shooting at Rippon Tor, which was near to the famous Haytor, where you can see the sea for 20 miles in three directions.

The fifties seemed a pleasant time for us, as we were a little better off than some. We had a 1938 Hillman Minx called 'Ela' and she was one of only two cars in the whole road. My father managed the Co-op butchers nearby and then took over the larger store in Hele. This meant that we had our fair share of sausages, faggots, liver and bacon. Occasionally we had a chicken on a Sunday and this was a real treat.

St Marychurch church after the bombing

TRIP TO ITALY

This was in 1964, when we were 14 and mad on pop music and pretty girls! Our elder brother worked at AEC in Southall and was able to get my father a discount on a new yellow Triumph Herald. What excitement! It had white rubber bumpers at the back. In September we set off for Folkstone to catch the ferry. It was my first ferry trip and unfortunately I spent most of the trip in the toilet!

We drove through North East France to Chalons-en-Champagne.

V FOR VICTORY

Whenever boys saw the car they did the 'V' for victory sign which made us feel very important. Dad had forgotten to put the black discs over the front headlights so we kept blinding oncoming motorists. In fact, the driver of a large Citroen behind us took particular exception to this and started flashing his lights at us. Colin didn't help matters when he turned around and gave the opposite 'V' sign to the driver!

We reached Brig, Switzerland the following evening and the smell of Fondue filled the hotel we were staying in. I pleaded that I could not eat it so he ordered the only alternative on the menu, steak and chips! He told me to buck up and be prepared to try foreign food and never forgot that my meal cost the same as three fondues!

LAKE GARDA

We arrived the next day in Northern Italy in a magical place called Sirmione, on the southern edge of Lake Garda. What a beautiful sight as you entered the small town over an actual drawbridge! We swam in the crystal clear lake with large fish all around us and the Dolomites as our backdrop. This was a really wonderful place and to really top it off we have a Morello cherry gelato. To our surprise, dad was speaking Italian to everyone; even in Venice he had a heated discussion with a Policeman who was trying to give him a parking ticket. After a few minutes of loud voices, the Policeman said "bravo!" and ripped the ticket up! We wondered what on Earth Dad had said to this Policeman, who was carrying a gun!

We stayed at Merano just outside of Venice and Dad ordered scampi for us. This was another amazing plate of tiny battered fish with fresh lemon. The next day we had another new taste experience, our first pizza. What with these delights and ice-cream to die for, we were becoming quite pro-Italian ourselves!

VERONA

We travelled back to Verona, where we dined at the home of the Secretary of Veronese Co-operative

Society. This was quite different for us to be at a formal dinner with food we had never tasted. Signor Menato spoke a little English, and his daughters, Paola and Maria joined in. Father said afterwards that Signor Menato had told him that he spoke Italian very well, but that it was the Italian of the peasants! On reflection, he was pleased to be associated with the Veronese peasants as they were the ones that had risked their lives for him.

VISIT TO ASPARETTO

We travelled 30km South of Verona to the small town of Asparetto and at first Dad had problems finding Marina's house. We visited the graveyard where we saw Marina's husbands grave and a photograph of him.

We found the farmhouse and were told by the new owners that Marina had moved to Vercelli, which is south west of Milan.

The people were very friendly and invited us in for drinks. They telephoned some local people and within 20 minutes about a dozen locals had turned up.

Several women ran across the farmyard to embrace my father, shouting "Davide, Davide!"

I was amazed at this, I was 14 and not used to seeing my father being so popular! His fluent Veronese had returned and they all chatted for an hour or so.

VISIT TO VERCELLI

The next day we set off to Vercelli. We arrived in the evening and stayed at the Savoy Hotel. I remember my father saying how expensive it was. However it was the only hotel in the town and so we had no choice.

MEETING MARINA

So we met Marina the next day in the apartment which had the most beautiful furniture in. She prepared a meal of rabbit, and Mario and Vernario joined us.

The brothers were so delighted to see my Dad; we had a tour of Vercelli and went to see where they worked.

Looking back it was a special experience to meet these three wonderful people. They had shared so much, with my Dad, the love and friendship was there forever.

We travelled back the next day, the car packed with olive oil, cheese and vino!

CHAPTER 23

RETURNING TO ITALY

It was 2011; we planned a trip to Italy to visit the places where my father had been a prisoner of war.

We flew into Naples and then decided not to visit LUCCA, Tuscany as the camp there had been a temporary camp with tents and a compound. We know this was a 'campo' and that Fred Riches was also taken there.

Our route took us from Frascati to Macerata, which is only 20 miles from the East Coast. We travelled through the 10km tunnel under the Apennines and reached Macerata in the afternoon. It was such a stunning city, in that, it was perched on top of a hill so that it stretched out across the skyline.

It looked similar to Carcassonne. The city had an opera house, a beautiful university building and striking piazzas. The next morning we visited the information centre and enquired about the prison camps. We were shown a map and some old photographs of one of the camps. They said that over 20,000 allied prisoners were held in these camps.

We travelled up the east coast staying at Pescaro and reached Mantova the next day. This too is a beautiful city. In front of it is a large lake which meets the city walls on the West side. This is one of the places my father was imprisoned from mid-April 1945.

It was market day and packed with people.

We had booked a cottage in the grounds of a large house in Asparetto.

The house was owned by a Countess and her son Carlo. He ran a tobacco production business, with over 1,000 hectares.

He found out where the farm was that my dad had lived in and arranged for us to visit this the next day.

We met the present owners of the house, who had been there since 1963.

This was now 2011, so I must have met them 47 years earlier!

They knew about the story and showed where the English POW's hid in the house and the hide out near the barn.

We sampled their home-made prosecco and left after an hour or so as life long friends!

PAINTINGS

While hiding in Marina's house in Asparetto, Ernest
Reed was able to produce some sketches and paintings.
Two of the watercolours have survived and are on the
walls of one of Marina's friends' houses in Asparetto

VISIT THE MAYOR

We visited the Town Hall in Cerea where we met the Deputy Mayor. We told him that we wished to present a plaque thanking the Italian people for their help to Allied prisoners.

They were very receptive and said that they would organise a reception for us the following week.

My daughter, Lucy's Italian is much better than mine and this was very helpful. We attended a Reception where we were presented with a ceramic picture and book of the area.

They told us that the plaque would be mounted in the Community Hall in Asparetto. The welcome was very friendly and I made a speech in Italian which had several grammatical mistakes. However as an Italian observer said it was delivered with 100% emotion.

On our return to England I became more determined than ever to write the book.

My Italian speech holding the plaque in the Mayor's office in Cerea

A LUCKY BREAK

Egidio Peptene lived in Asparetto and remembers the English POW's. He is now 84, he recalled that David spoke good Italian and that Fredrico was a baker and the people from the village used to bring flour to the house.

In 2012 we had an email out of the blue from Wendy, asking if I was the son of David Robillard. It turned out that her father was Fred Riches from Norfolk, who was a fellow escapee.

Wendy said that she had been trying to trace the family with whom her father had stayed.

We met near Norwich in August 2013 and she was able to produce letters from my father sent to her Dad. These were dated in 1945 and it was obvious that they were real friends.

What was really great was that she had established a link with Marina's family, plus she had several photographs of the POW's and the family.

This was the break I needed and since then we have been exchanged information. We met again in Bracciano, which is north of Rome, with Stella Leardini the niece of Marina and friends from Verona. Their help has been so important in recording these events for prosperity.

Egidio and Wendy, the daughter of Fred Riches

From left to right, top line David, Redorna, Mario, Marina, Giovanni and Ernest

Front row, Les, Venerio with the dog Tanike

The backdrop is a field of maize taken summer 1944

Per Davide; il mio nonno.

Carino nonno,

Mi manchi tanto e vorrei che potessimo avere più tempo insieme.

Spesso la strada è rotta e la sua molto difficile decidere cosa fare nella vita. Però hai dato a noi una lezione molto molto importante che dopo un sacca di cose brutte è possibile trovare ancora la compassione, coraggio ed fede. Voi e il popolo di Asparetto sono le persone più coraggiose che abbia mai conosciuto. Anche se non sei più qui la tua storia sarà in diretta su.

Ci hai insegnato ad apprezzare la vita e non mollare mai. Per questo, la vita è bella.

Ti amo.

xx